31

DISCIPLINES

OF HIGHLY

SUCCESSFUL

CREATIVES

A daily dose of inspiration to sharpen your creative edge

BY NOAH ELIAS

DEDICATION

This book is dedicated to Chantel, Griffin and Noah, who are my crew in this amazing adventure of life. I don't have enough words to say how much I love you and how thankful I am for you.

Thanks to my amazing team: Jared, Lauren, Kellie, Lefty and Des, who are the most loyal and dedicated partners I could ask for; Dave and Christy for putting wind in our sail; my mentors: Bob Shank, Dave Carder, and Ryan Audagnotti, who have faithfully helped me sharpen my saw and remind me of my true identity.

Table of Contents

Introd

uction

HELLO MY FRIEND

As an entrepreneur, your life is packed with managing and stewarding the responsibilities you have in life, business, and family, all while creating amazing ideas and initiatives. It is a very tall order to be self-employed without losing your mind and soul in the process. Even more, if you are a creative, what you are fashioning arises from your heart. Producing amazing work while managing all the other dynamics of life can be overwhelming. It can feel like you're trying to draw a sketch while sitting in a boat that is surrounded by a tornado; this lifestyle requires a strong stomach. And that is why I wrote this book.

This book that you hold in your hand contains over 30 years of lessons and successes as a creative entrepreneur while raising a family and having an impact on the world. In these pages, I share the realities and underbelly of what it takes to risk, fail, and risk again. The topics have been selected because they are the most common themes that continue to surface in life: business, relationships, family, fear, failure, and risk.

My hope is that you will take the knowledge and information found in these pages and put them into practice in your marriage, with your kids, in your business, and in relationships.

Some have asked if this is a faith-based book. If you've followed me for a while, you'll know that I base my life decisions on the sound wisdom of biblical principles, and it's impossible for me to share my learnings without also sharing the biblical truths discovered. So, you will see some peppered throughout these pages. However, I can tell you this: The most profound wisdom, discernment, and knowledge have all stemmed from the root of divine influence.

How to use this book //

Each morning you wake up to embark on a new day that adds a page to the story of your life. Therefore, my intention was to create a book that would provide you with a dose of wisdom to muse over while you drink your morning coffee and practical, applicable steps you can put into play. Each day is a devotion to read and digest. However, I would strongly encourage you to rinse and repeat the readings over and over. The moment you finish, start again. The knowledge will then take root in your heart, and these new disciplines will become second nature.

What you believe changes your actions. Your actions become disciplines, and those disciplines will result in healthy change and peace of mind.

I'm in your corner,

NOAH

1

Managing Expectations

MANAGING EXPECTATIONS

Do you find yourself beginning each day with a list of to-dos in your head and plans to accomplish them? Do you also find that you become cranky, unsettled, or upset when the list doesn't get accomplished, or worse yet, when someone throws an unexpected task into the middle of your already busy day?

Here's the deal: There is an unseen force in our heads that radically impacts our view of the world, the people around us, and even ourselves. It's called expectations. Being disciplined and mastering your expectations will radically change your life.

Here's an example: You are going through your day managing all the details and responsibilities. Unexpected interruptions start to happen. All of a sudden things go sideways and feel out of control. The disruptions can be anything from an unexpected flat tire on the way to dropping your kid off at school to someone not showing up to a meeting. Or how about setting off on a family vacation, going surfing, or visiting a friend? You commit to these engagements only to find out that the hotel wasn't what you were hoping for, the swell was lousy, or the friend you hoped to visit didn't make the get-together a priority.

Our peace and joy are often determined by our expectations. Imagine a scale with two sides: on one side is expectation, and on the other side is peace and joy. If our expectations are super high, our peace and joy are low. If we lower our expectations, our peace and joy are super high.

I know this concept is super simple, but it can and will have a profound impact on your day and your life. Your internal self-talk is one of the most powerful forces and can either break you or build you. Imagine an internal bully kicking your a** every hour. The messages this bully carries are "you should be farther in this endeavor" or "you should have more money by now" or "you should be losing more weight" or "you should be more in control" or "you should better at this by now." Bottom line, you are "should'ing" all over yourself.

If you can become disciplined in mastering your expectations, you will elevate to a level of peace and joy that is more than you can imagine. Here's why: Unmet expectations that are out of alignment lead to anger. And anger, if left untreated, will cause you to be harsh and punchy, with no control over yourself. More important, the fallout of anger leaves a wake of destruction in the relationships around you. I've witnessed business owners lose clients simply because they couldn't keep their emotions in check during negotiations.

The mouth echoes the heart. What we say and how we say it exposes the condition of our hearts. And anger often means we aren't getting something we want. So, it can be a useful road-map to get us where we need to be and reveal to us what we need to get rid of.

I'll confess a personal expectation that once triggered anger in me. We have a family of four and two dogs in our house. I have a private office and studio on our property that allows me the awesome luxury of working from home. One of the things I love is a clean house and things orderly and organized. Whenever my family members left things out or didn't clean up, I'd have an internal dialogue that went something like this: "They don't care about this house and these things;" "These kids should know how to keep a house clean and remember to put their stuff away;" "If they loved me, they would remember and take time to clean." WOW! I spent so much of my life out of whack with unrealistic expectations trying to control my environment. Ultimately, my self-talk said, "They aren't cleaning, and we are losing control. You are a parent out of control." So, I started keeping an inventory of expectations. And I began communicating, with respect, my concerns and requests for a tidy house. It's taken me a while to learn this, but it's not about those around me. I'm the one who needs work.

Our family members, employees, or friends will not want to work with or for us if we use fear, anger, and a hot temper to make our requests. Keep in mind, a fool gives vent to his anger. He is out of control, undisciplined, and is operating from a place of being wounded. But if you can adopt the discipline of diagnosing your expectations and find the root of your anger, peace and joy will be the result because you will be operating with grace and compassion. And this will not only apply to those around you, but to yourself as well.

If we answer anger with anger, we give way to answering a fool according to his folly. We become the fool too. It's a lose/lose.

Challenge: Take a quick inventory: Write down in your journal or on a piece of paper what angers you the most. Or, think about what areas in your life you wish to change for the better. Then write down your expectation about the circumstance. Are they realistic? Are you showing grace toward yourself? Are your expectations way off? Ask your friends and loved ones. Would they say you are a hot head or cool and calm in your responses? Do you find that you react emotionally to everything and use the excuse that you're "passionate" about it?

The discipline of mastering expectations is one very few possess. You can either react to life or you can respond to it.

Have an amazing day!

A gentle answer turns away wrath, but a harsh word stirs up anger.
- PROVERBS 15:1 NASB

This you know, my beloved brethren. But everyone must be quick to hear, slow to speak and slow to anger. **- JAMES 1:19 NASB**

He who is slow to anger has great understanding, but he who is quick-tempered exalts folly. **- PROVERBS 14:29 NASB**

He who is slow to anger is better than the mighty, and he who rules his spirit, than he who captures a city. **- PROVERBS 16:32 NASB**

He who restrains his words has knowledge, and he who has a cool spirit is a man of understanding. **- PROVERBS 17:27**

Do you see a man who is hasty in his words? There is more hope for a fool than for him. **- PROVERBS 29:20**

2 Overcoming Fear Is Essential to Grow

OVERCOMING FEAR IS ESSENTIAL TO GROW

There was a season in my life when I realized my responsibilities were growing. The risks and rewards in business were building. I don't know if you have ever felt this way, overcome by the responsibilities of marriage, parenting, and career. We try to advance in all areas of life equally, but our default usually is our career.

As life levels up, we can become paralyzed by fear. We experience the fear of losing everything we've worked for. We worry about doing something, anything to mess things up. But this fear blunts our creativity. We end up taking fewer risks because we have so much at stake.

Here's an example. Maybe you're a blogger who is finally making some money and gaining good momentum. Your platform is strong but you don't want to rock the boat. You have a desire in your gut to live more authentically but you're scared to be yourself due to the fear of loss of connection, loss of belonging, acceptance, and love. It's funny—we can build the empires we spent years dreaming about only to find that they've become a birdcage.

My friend, here's the deal: You will never change the world or the lives in your home if you continue to play small. You must be willing to punch fear in face and overcome the lies you're telling yourself. In the beginning of starting your company, learning to parent, or learning to be a good spouse, you were like a professional high-diver. You would climb to new and higher dives, jumping off without fear. But at some level, the height got to you. You decided you didn't want to lose anything you had built, and you allowed fear to run the show. But what would your life, business, marriage, or parenting look like if you started climbing and jumping once more? What if you began raising the height again?

The successful entrepreneurs I encounter have developed the discipline of being fearless. They have mastered the art of shoving past themselves when they stand in their own way. This is a huge discipline to implement, probably one of the most important I know.

Tip: One of the biggest breakthroughs I had was when I finally understood that things aren't what they seem. We build up circumstances in our heads, and they always appear much bigger and scarier in our minds than what they really are. This is the double-edged sword of creative thinking, when your amazing superhero power gets used in the wrong way: on yourself.

When we encounter this fear, the goal is to diffuse the situation, circumstance, or challenge by looking it in the face as soon as possible. See your situation for what it is and allow truth to shine through. When you do that, productivity will flow.

A big part of this is accepting the fact that you've allowed yourself to be driven and run by fear rather than truth and love. Give yourself some grace. Offer yourself forgiveness because the dread you feel is an instinct inside all of us. Think back to the high-diver scenario. When you walk to the end of the board, your body might be "all in" with jumping, but your head will throw up all of this doubt and fear out of self-preservation. This is being human, so cut yourself some slack and keep moving forward.

Overcoming fear is a discipline like all others. It gains strength each time you use it.

Challenge: Take out your journal or a notepad. Write down the fears that are at the forefront of your mind. Keep asking yourself what negative self-talk and lies you hear the most in your head throughout the day. What specific lie or fear do you continually hear week in and week out?

My own take: Let me get personal on this one. Fear ran my life for a great many years. I eventually wrote a book on it called #Fearhunters because I wanted to help people break free and live out their calling. My personal take is this: God has placed me on this earth to accomplish an assignment and a mission. The mission I am carrying out happens to be in enemy territory. The enemy is doing everything possible to take me out. The enemy's goal is to make me focus on my identity and who I am "not." His job is to persecute me and tear me down with lies. He uses fear to keep me from being unproductive. If I'm unproductive, then I can't help people in this world and show them God's love. Know this, the closer you move toward your calling, the greater the interference will be. Expect it.

Your greatest growth and impact lie on the other side of your greatest fear.

Today, you get to pick how your day will go. Fear can run you or you can dismantle it with truth. You might be dreading a phone call with a client or vendor this week. What's the worst-case scenario? What's the truth? Like we discussed, fear is natural and expected. You fear the outcome if you are real in your marriage, kids, and relationships. What if today, you made small steps to overcoming your fear in order to grow into being who you truly are?

Perfect love casts out fear. Love yourself by being true to yourself and others. Otherwise, you run the risk of being a poser and faking it. Develop the discipline of knowing how to dismantle fear. It isn't going away anytime soon. But you can become a master of not being owned by it.

Danger will always be present in life, but fear is optional. In order to grow, we must overcome. To overcome, we must have the discipline to deal with fear. Are you having challenges with your creativity, your launches, and building new ideas? Do you become easily paralyzed? If you need help with removing fear and shame from your life, check out my book **(www. fearhuntersbook.com)**, as it will give you freedom to step boldly into your leadership.

Have an amazing day.

3

Know Thy Calling

KNOW THY CALLING

once heard a saying that went something like this, "In order to have a calling, one must know the caller." In my experience, the most influential entrepreneurs have a laser-like focus on their calling—it is their True North, their plumb line in life.

You may be reading this but not knowing your calling; or you might even think you don't have one. My hope is that today's reading will help you to discover your calling and challenge you in your approach to it.

Focusing on your calling requires you to have the discipline to first ascertain what it is and then chase after it ... relentlessly. Here are some practical steps you can take to determine and pursue your calling over your lifetime.

Whether you believe in God or not, I would love for you to hear what I've learned and what my journey has been like in regard to this topic. For many, this will be your first exposure to these truths.

First, I believe your calling is so unique that it will not be lived out or completed by anyone before you or after you. God designed you specifically, "on purpose." You aren't just a natural byproduct of your parents or an accident. You are God's workmanship created to do amazing things. He prepared these things in advance before you were born.

Second, like Superman, I believe that you've been sent here on a mission. You have an assignment that has been wired into you. The fun part is that you get to discover what your assignment is. One of the ways you can discern your calling is by aligning your unique talents, abilities, and the influence you have on bringing people to God's love. These three areas make up the DNA of your calling.

Third, you will find that you are living in your calling when it feels natural and you would do it for free. In other words, you will feel like you're working the least amount while producing the greatest value. Take these gifts of grace and love to others and bring people into eternity.

Jesus had a specific calling on His life. The day I realized what it was, my calling became clear. If I am going to follow His example and leadership, then it's more than likely my calling will mirror His.

So, how does that apply to you and me in terms of our gifts and creativity? I'll make it simple. We are all called to love God, love people, and make disciples. "How" we do that is up to us. God gave each one of us the beautiful gift of choice—we choose how to live and what to do. What He really cares about is that we do it together to help bring people to His love and populate heaven. And best of all, He wants us to have a blast while doing it.

People will often ask about the inspiration behind my initiatives and painting ideas. Here's my answer: When you partner with the Creator of this universe, you get supernatural results. God is the owner of my life, my wife, my kids, and my companies, as well as all of my relationships. They are on loan to me, and every breath I take is a gift of His grace. That said, when you know your calling, who your Caller is, and why you're doing what you're doing, the "how" becomes easy.

The most influential entrepreneurs I know navigate their time on this earth by living with the end in mind and ordering their days accordingly.

Love God, love people, make disciples, and use your creativity to do it.

Have a great day!

Many are the plans in a person's heart, but it is the LORD's purpose that prevails.
- **PROVERBS 19:21 NIV**

The mind of man plans his way, but the LORD directs his steps.
- **PROVERBS 16:9 NASB**

1

Chase Impact, Not Income

CHASE IMPACT, NOT INCOME

I t was a beautiful afternoon as I sat with an entrepreneur who had grown his business to a multi-million dollar level. I wanted to know about the highs and lows of his thirty-year career. We talked about everything from product development to production, hiring and staffing to customers. But out of all the topics we discussed, there was one that captured his attention more than any other. Can you guess what it was?

Money. When we started to talk about it, his eyes lit up like a child's on Christmas morning. I think many entrepreneurs can relate to this. When you work for yourself, it is very easy to define your success and even define yourself based on how much money you produce.

But troubles come when we base our self-worth on our net worth.

Here's how to avoid this trap. Focus the meaning of your business on making a positive impact. What does this mean? The best way I can describe it is to be a professional "giver." When you are a professional giver, your goal and meaning is to bless others with your abundance.

Your business is a tool and a means to an end. If the business is the only end, then it is successful but not significant. Providing for our family is the baseline but not the end goal. You didn't become an entrepreneur just to create a job for yourself. You create businesses to generate a profit, and from these profits, help others profit who struggle to create profit for themselves.

Tip: If you are in business for yourself, how much of your revenue is going to healing the world? Our business became a tool to rescue AIDS orphans in South Africa and has provided a home for eight children plus all of their medical and dental needs. This home will provide care until they reach adulthood. Our company culture has shifted from getting to giving. The motivation to get out of bed must go beyond a paycheck. It's essential.

All entrepreneurs hope to get past just surviving. I think most of us believe that success is the ultimate destination. But the wise go beyond success and focus on the road to significance. Therein lies the land of true wealth, freedom, and eternal impact. It has little to do with the dollar value of your business.

Discipline yourself to continually take stock of where and how you can lead your efforts to make an impact, not just income.

Have an amazing day.

5

Don't Wait for Inspiration to Create and Launch

DON'T WAIT FOR INSPIRATION
TO CREATE AND LAUNCH

The benefit of being a creative entrepreneur is that you possess not only the abilities to visualize and dream, but also to execute those ideas and bring them to life. These are amazing superhero powers that very few people have. But they are not results, in and of themselves. You have to use them! We all know that thinking about writing a book or thinking about creating a song isn't the same as actually sitting down and writing, painting, or making music.

One of the potential blind spots for creatives that can stunt your growth is only creating when you feel like it. If you only create under perfect circumstances, you will only be doing your craft twenty percent of the time. But the good news is that you can transform this particular blind spot into one of your greatest strengths, and in the days ahead, I will be giving you practical steps to do exactly that.

Remember the honeymoon phase of launching your first business idea? Your first book? What about your first series of art? You had a spark of inspiration. You started to venture out on the journey of creating tangible results and bringing ideas and dreams to reality. If your inspiration had a level from one to ten, you were at twenty!

But over time—especially if you have been creating in your trade for years—it feels like it takes an enormous amount of effort to recreate that same level of inspiration. Your creative tank feels low, and more effort is required to get excited. Your feeling of being "into it" has faded. You may even feel like you're "forcing it." The potential blind spot here is that if you don't feel inspired, you don't create.

Tip: I want to encourage you to base your creativity, your dreams, and execution on a principle, not on a feeling. Here's an example of this principle in action: There are days when husbands or wives don't "feel" like loving their spouse. But being married means that a husband or wife must honor the vow and commit to loving each other regardless of circumstances or feelings. Why? Because love isn't a feeling. It's an action.

In order to be successful, your creativity and leadership as an entrepreneur deserves to be honored the same way you would honor a marriage. You made a commitment to yourself, your creativity, and your dreams. If you only do the work when you feel creative, it won't happen.

I've learned two things about this principle over the years. First, I've discovered that eighty percent of my days are spent doing things I don't "feel" like doing. The other twenty percent is doing what comes naturally and flows like second nature.

Second, I've learned that if I show up to do the work and invest the precious time that has been gifted to me today, inspiration will show up to meet me.

You only find gold if you dig.

Action: Grab your journal and answer these questions: What would you do if you knew you would not fail at it? What is the roadblock? Do you only create and do the work when inspired? What has been the result in the past when you showed up to get things done regardless of how you felt?

The true entrepreneurs who have the grit to show up and produce results are those who don't allow circumstances, relationship dynamics, or weather conditions to hinder them from creating. They often create in spite of their feelings.

It's easy to do the work when you're in love and on the beginning of your journey. True love, passion, and wisdom reveal themselves when you're years in, weathering yet another storm, without any clear sense of direction. When that happens, you have the opportunity to be one of the few who will rise above all circumstances to create results. You'll be at a level of creativity and output that only a few entrepreneurs produce. This is how you turn a blind spot into what could be your greatest strength.

You've got this! Have an amazing day!

6

Actively Pursue Wisdom and Sharpen Your Axe

ACTIVELY PURSUE WISDOM AND SHARPEN YOUR AXE

A woodsman was once asked, 'What would you do if you had just five minutes to chop down a tree?' He answered, 'I would spend the first two and a half minutes sharpening my axe.' - ANONYMOUS

I often see men and women in positions of authority—managers, parents, business owners, freelancers, and artists—trying to operate their lives as solo leaders. They courageously attack roadblocks, problem-solve with Google, deal with curve balls, and attempt to navigate their day-to-day life independently. For reasons that are their own, they choose not to seek outside advice. They simply don't know how or where to find sources of wisdom to help them on their journey.

If this is the case for you, you may find yourself feeling lost and asking the same questions every day: "Am I doing the right thing? Is this the best solution to the problem I'm facing? Are my choices wise?" You constantly second-guess yourself and your decisions. You feel the weight of the world on your shoulders without any relief in sight from the pressure. But you don't want to waste energy looking for a mentor or guide, especially if you're not 100 percent sure it will be worth your time and effort.

I know the feeling all too well. Trying to do life, run a business, or raise children in this kind of vacuum is not only time-consuming, difficult, and frustrating, it is also incredibly lonely. You have to face every new hurdle on your own, problem-solve, and figure out a solution. There is no sounding board to bounce ideas off of. There's no guide to shine a light on the stumbling blocks you might encounter, no one with tried-and-tested solutions.

Whatever the journey, doing it on your own is like trying to march up Mount Everest and just "wing it." That would be beyond foolish. If you

ACTIVELY PURSUE WISDOM AND SHARPEN YOUR AXE

were going to trek up the famous Himalayan Mountains, you would talk to as many people as possible—those who have actually successfully made the climb—to glean from their wisdom, experience, and advice.

The same is true in life. You absolutely need guides. You need help. You need sharpening. The most highly effective entrepreneurs are those who don't just follow themselves. Scripture is clear about this too. "Where there is no guidance the people fall, but in abundance of counselors there is victory" (Proverbs 11:14 NASB).

For leaders and entrepreneurs, having a mentor or a guide is non-negotiable, in my opinion. In fact, I consider it a prerequisite. If you want to climb to certain heights of success, having a guide is absolutely essential.

Without a mentor, many entrepreneurs, parents, and leaders get eaten alive. What's worse is that it's easy to get discouraged when looking at people who are already at the summit. You see them in magazines and watch their lives on social media. But you never truly know the cost, sacrifices, strategies, and devotion required to get the results.

Here are two of the most important strategies that I use to get out of this sort of vacuum:

- **Actively pursue wisdom:** This means taking a proactive approach to finding people who are wiser and more experienced than you. For an artist, that could be a former teacher or a more experienced peer. For a parent, that could be a grandparent, in-law, or someone whose parenting you admire and respect.

- **Sharpen your axe:** Sharpening your axe means investing your time in improving your skill set, knowledge, and expertise. This could be reading a book, taking a class, spending quality time by yourself, or (for tired parents), just taking a nap. Sharpening your axe means taking the time to improve yourself in a strategic way that enriches your life, work, and hobbies. Look to deep friendships—those who will pour into you and refill your cup. Be intentional.

Action: Today, maybe even right now, take a moment to ask yourself these questions: What was the last book you read or listened to that helped you sharpen your axe? Who are the mentors in your life that you actually carve out time to spend time with, ask questions, and learn from? Who is in your up-line that is willing to pass on wisdom? When you are with people who appear to be "catching up to you" in their expertise or knowledge, do you write them off, or do you look to see what you can learn? What specific area(s) would be most strategic to invest time in and sharpen your axe? What are your greatest areas of weakness that need improving? Who can you reach out to today to establish a mentor relationship, one who will help you detect your blind spots and find hidden value in you?

Have an amazing day!

You don't become extraordinary under the influence of ordinary people.
- BOB SHANK

For by wise guidance you will wage war, and in abundance of counselors there is victory. **- PROVERBS 24:6 NASB**

The way of a fool is right in his own eyes, but a wise man is he who listens to counsel. **- PROVERBS 12:15 NASB**

7

Don't Settle for the Status Quo

DON'T SETTLE FOR
THE STATUS QUO

O ne of the biggest realities of being a creative entrepreneur is the fact that you're a pioneer. The definition of a pioneer is a person who is among the first to explore or settle a new country or area. It's also said that they develop or are the first to use and apply a new method, area of knowledge, or activity.

But being a pioneer comes with a steep cost. That cost is leaving the comfort zone of the status quo. Exploring new areas means encountering new challenges, roadblocks, and discomforts.

But successful entrepreneurs push through. They stay curious, search for new ways to teach, and continue to look beyond the horizon. They embrace getting out of their comfort zone. They thrive when they leave the familiar.

Our culture is obsessed with the status quo. You will find no shortage of followers who do everything possible to keep things comfortable and predictable. The only problem is that there isn't much risk or growth, personally or in your career. If you are planning on pioneering new territories in business and relationships, then you can be sure of one thing: You will be in an unpredictable environment almost all of the time.

If you are cranky and surprised in your current circumstances, I would encourage you to evaluate your expectations. It should not surprise you that as an entrepreneur, you inhabit a hostile, unpredictable environment. You should not expect things to be all sunshine and green pastures. Risk and leaving the status quo has a price of admission—being uncomfortable. But as we all know, the upside is so good and worth it. You discover new ways, hidden value, new products, and new opportunities. Don't settle for anything less.

Tip: Today, you have the opportunity to pioneer and abandon the comfort of the status quo. Does that opportunity excite you or terrify you? Why? Write about it and talk about it with friends and family.

Action: Grab your journal. Ask yourself a couple of questions: If I could launch a dream and knew I wouldn't fail, what would it be? How much of this year is the same as last year? Am I playing life safe trying to get things secure in money and possessions? Or am I following inspiration from God and my heart to play in the sandbox of my mind to build exciting dreams? If I asked my closest friends, would they say that I am playing life small or going big? Here's two other big questions. Am I judging myself based on how many ideas and dreams I have? Am I hiding behind dreams and ideas by not actually launching anything? Am I a poser wearing the costume of "doer" but living inside of a terrified dreamer?

My friend, life is too short to blend in to the status quo. You were made for more. Don't settle for anything less.

Have an amazing day!

———————————————

8

Your Greatest Asset

YOUR GREATEST ASSET

When you contemplate the millions of companies and personalities around the world, you can start to see the constant barrage of messages forced on us every day through TV, radio, and media. Furthermore, technology continues to scale, forcing us to see near-constant messaging. If you don't agree with me, try these experiments: take a drive in your car without listening to anything. Better yet, try not using your phone for a day. What I'm getting at is we live in a very noisy world.

But the human mind is very clever in the way that it processes and digests information. I'm going to show you how you can leverage the brain's subconscious "cleverness" to your advantage.

Each person wakes up every day with his or her mind running in "comfort mode," sort of like autopilot. You get out of bed, do your routine, then rinse and repeat, every single day. However, underneath this autopilot mode is a constant subconscious process that is scanning, looking, and searching for anomalies. The definition of anomaly is "something that deviates from what is standard, normal, or expected." Therefore, our minds naturally and automatically scan for something that is remarkable.

If you are aware that this is happening in the minds of your potential customers, you can intentionally structure the landscape of your marketing to harness this natural curiosity. You can easily become an advertising ninja with Jedi-like instincts.

So how do you do this? One word: Story.

Since the beginning of time, story has been the DNA of the human's heart. God wrote each of our unique stories into His greater story. The most successful creative entrepreneurs tap into this supernatural power. Smart entrepreneurs don't sell, they share. Sharing your message through story will always trump marketing.

Thriving creative entrepreneurs have the ability to share through story. Whether you are writing a blog post, sharing on social media how you baked an incredible apple pie, or selling a car, the secret is crafting a genuine story.

Tip: Analyze the posts you have on social media. Do you see anything worth sharing or anything that tells a story? Or is it just eye candy? What if I told you that your story can change lives and impact people? What if there is someone struggling with depression or pain today who, if you shared what is on your heart, might be encouraged and lifted above their circumstances?

Take your sales, marketing, pitch decks, and products to the world via story. Pull back the curtain of your life. Let people see how you make it and why you make it, and be real. The world is filled with posers. Be you. We need you.

Your story is your greatest asset. How often are you sharing it, using it, and scaling it?

Have an amazing day!

9

The Power of Your Story

THE POWER OF YOUR STORY

O ne of the best disciplines I see in leaders and business owners is the ability to stay true to their story. Our story contains not only our greatest gift to the world, but it is also connected to our deep "why." Companies that lead without knowing their "why" will be very busy fighting the war without knowing who or what they are fighting for. When a leader disciplines herself to know her story, it acts as a compass to stay on track for her life calling.

Here's how this applies in my life and business. During my childhood, I encountered challenges and experienced wounds. Instead of hiding these wounds, I began leveraging these stories and weaving them into my message, brand, and the products I sell. What was the net effect? Clarity of purpose and my calling in life regarding my family and business.

In short, your story is your greatest asset.

Whether you're working a corporate job, running a restaurant, writing a children's book, or blogging each week, your personal story is the DNA of what makes your platform and product so impactful on the lives around you. Do you think your story is too embarrassing or one you'd rather not tell? I've got some insight to help you take what's happened and turn it into gold!

Your story possesses the solution to help someone else break through a problem or challenge.

Why don't you share your true authentic self with others through your business? What are you afraid of? Your mind is probably throwing up all kinds of walls in self-defense to try to shut you down. But I've got GREAT news for you and a step-by-step checklist for you to use in your daily approach. This is a game changer on how you can leverage the good, the bad, and the ugly of your life to be a solution to someone's greatest challenge.

The Power of Your Story to Reach Others

1. Your story is your greatest asset. How often are you meeting new people and leveraging your story or bio to reach and connect with new acquaintances?

2. Your biggest traumas, hurts, and failures can actually help others. The more you stay quiet, the fewer the people who will get help.

3. If you are resistant to sharing your story, are you spending time talking with friends and mentors who could help you grow in your boldness?

Hindrances to Sharing Your Story

1. Do you feel embarrassed?

Tip: Use social media to experiment with how you tell your story; this will help you to overcome any fears you may have. Maybe you dealt with failure in a sport. Share the event, its impact, and how you overcame. Then share and ask others for comments and input.

2. Do you have a fear of rejection?

Tip: We often base our decisions off what other people think and say about us. If you find you are worried about these things, you aren't living your life. You are living theirs.

3. Do you feel ill-equipped or unqualified?

Tip: Listen, we are all broken. We all play the game of life with scars and battle wounds. However, that shouldn't keep us from playing. If we wait until we reach perfection or readiness, we will never launch or share our stories.

Lastly, here are couple thoughts to consider in your approach to life and business.

Look for a need and fill it. Your story possesses valuable gold. It can help release other people into incredible freedom. I used to be scared about walking on stage to speak, but when I realized how many people needed help and wanted to hear what I had to share, everything changed. Stop thinking about your perceived lack of preparation. Instead, start thinking about what you have NOW and how it could solve someone's problem.

Your life is a blank canvas. You get to choose today how the rest of your life will be painted. Maybe your past was a horror. Maybe it was traumatic and ugly. Maybe it was a thriller.

Whatever the case, you can't change your past, but you can paint your future. Paint away and share that image with the world.

Have an amazing day!

———————————

10

Create Systems

CREATE SYSTEMS

Think about the brands you encounter on a daily basis. These brands include restaurants, stores, coffee shops, theme parks, your barber or hair stylist, car wash, bill pay service, bank, and most of your online experiences. Now, think of the overall experience you have each time you interact with that brand. A few things might come to mind that combine to create that experience: the look, feel, the voice they use to communicate, how easy or hard it is to finalize the transaction. Some brands have amazing customer experiences and others miss the mark. What is essential to building a world-class business?

As an entrepreneur, you are boldly stepping into risk, building and innovating new ideas. Eventually, the goal is to build these ideas into profitable and meaningful businesses. Most creative entrepreneurs can dream up amazing ideas and fill journals with intentions. But they lack the disciplines needed to bring them into reality successfully.

This book is a collection of disciplines that can help you get from dreams to realities. One of the key disciplines to becoming a successful entrepreneur is the idea of creating systems within your business. Systems are necessary for healthy growth and measurable outcomes. Systems provide a tremendous amount of security, automation, and predictability as well.

In *The E-Myth Revisited*, written by Michael Gerber, he stresses the importance of systems in your business and building a franchise model for structuring your business and life. I would highly suggest you buy the book and read it once a year for the rest of your life.

There is nothing better than being able to focus on your craft, knowing that in the background your business is structured, smart, and effective because you've created powerful systems. Having this structure provides a feeling of safety and ease so you can create freely.

One of the most important components of your systems should include the ability to accurately measure results. Gathering data on sales, ad performance statistics, and engagement levels allows you to see and measure the realities of how efficient and successful your business is. Fools judge life, themselves, and others on intentions. Wise business owners can prove success in actual, measurable results.

Challenge: Do you currently have a brand bible created so that if you or any of your team were to leave, someone could pick up the brand bible and fill that role? Are your advertising, hiring, and sales all based on a step-by-step process? Do you feel your business is structured or is it based on outside behaviors and the actions of others? You owe it to yourself, your family, and your customers to operate in structured systems. Everyone will experience peace of mind when you have put systems in place. If you don't, you will spend your valuable time managing chaos. So ask yourself, what happens when a person visits my website, store, or tries to book a call with me? Are the steps different every time or are the steps predictable?

Your success as a creative entrepreneur, along with the scaling of your life and career, are determined by how disciplined you are in creating the systems that will get you there. Systems become predictable, and when those systems become predictable, they can be measurable.

Action step: Very few entrepreneurs invest in the discipline of systems. Look at your week and take inventory: Are my days set? Do I set my time and schedule, or are they determined by others? Do I have projected goals for this month, quarter, or year? Does my business have systems in place and a brand bible? Do my proposals, contracts, and billing all have a system? Do I have dashboards and spreadsheets to measure?

Have an amazing day!

11

Early Bird Gets the Worm

EARLY BIRD GETS THE WORM

O ver the last thirty years of my career, I've found that I am most productive during the early mornings, *well* before sunrise. Most successful entrepreneurs have developed the discipline of getting up early and living a full day before everyone else even gets up. This discipline might be one of the most vital, but it requires planning. Let me present a few benefits of being an early riser.

Let's say your kids normally get up at 7 a.m. If you were to wake at 4:30 a.m., you would have an average of 2.5 hours of focused, uninterrupted time.

Benefit: Focused time produces a higher quality of work. The 2.5 hours can be an investment in a new body of work, a new book, or creating new content.

One of the most important benefits is the fact that you aren't just gaining another 15-20 hours per week, you are creating something valuable during that time. Think about it: that's 80 extra hours per month, 960 hours per year. So when people tell me they don't have any time because they are raising kids, have a job, etc., I tell them they suffer from wasting time.

Here's how to execute this. First, set yourself up for success the night before. Get yourself into bed at a time that will give you the sleep you need. We all need different amounts of sleep. If you have to, set an alarm to be in bed by a certain time. You will notice within about ten days that your body will switch to autopilot. Yes, you will actually shift from being a night owl to a morning person. I know you will fight this like crazy, but take a look below at the insane benefits from doing this.

Second, save television, movies, and entertainment for the weekends only. Use your evenings to be with family. Then settle yourself down to read and "land the plane" by getting your mind and body ready to sleep. I notice my creativity and mind are on such a high level all day that I could go to sleep by eight o'clock every night. So much happens in my day, and it is super concentrated. When you wake up early, you will go into a mode of thinking that is crystal clear. Here's what I found: You start the day with a full tank and can begin fresh without distraction, media, or devices. Focused work will produce the best ideas and the best quality.

Side note: I've found that the discoveries I make in prayer and the breakthroughs that happen with my creativity all occur during these early hours. As I look back, I often wonder what would have happened had I not been up and in that moment? I would have missed the gold waiting for me.

I've encountered hundreds of people who fight this idea. They tell me that they could never do it. They insist that they are evening people. I have to disagree. When you have to fight for a quiet space during your day, you lose energy and willpower to fight off distraction and interruption. By the end of the day, you are fried and have very little in the tank to begin a brand new task. I suggest going to bed the same time every night so your body is aware and falls into the routine.

My routine looks something like this: I wake up and spend one hour in the living room with lights off and fireplace on. Candle lit. Silence. This time is for prayer and dreaming up ideas with God. Then I move into capturing these ideas and prayers in my journal.

Then I move into super deep work like writing or painting. I wrap it up with working out. So, before 9 a.m., I have accomplished more than most people do in eight hours.

I don't have any distractions or threats of interruption—just peaceful creativity, freedom to think, and no anxiety. You'll be amazed. You'll feel like your days are a vacation. I have been able to do this while we had newborns in the house and were running multiple companies and initiatives.

Think of the total extra hours you will gain each morning with a full tank, no distractions, and absolute focus. What quality of work will you create? How many more initiatives can be accomplished in this time? By living your day like this, you will add three to four more lifetimes of quality work in the mornings. Think about it. It's incredible what you will create in these mornings.

Have an amazing day.

12

Hack
Your Email &
Social Media

HACK YOUR EMAIL & SOCIAL MEDIA

Rarely have I ever met successful entrepreneurs who weren't in charge of their time, tools, and systems. They seem to be in the driver's seat of life as it pertains to their calendars, phones, and self-imposed boundaries.

The greatest boundary I learned pertains to email and social media. In Tim Ferriss' book, *The 4-Hour Workweek*, he explains the idea of disciplining yourself to email once a day and then, after you master that, once a week. The discipline fascinated me. I realized how addicted to my devices I was. Here is what I learned and what you will probably learn as well if you implement this discipline. But first, let's talk about the discipline itself.

The idea is to limit checking your email until noon and then again at 4 p.m. By doing this, you will be free to focus on producing higher quality work in a fraction of the time. We live in an extremely noisy and distracting world. It is going to continue to become louder and filled with more messages competing for your time and attention. This is why I call email and social media "time bandits."

The greatest threat: One of the greatest tragedies I see is when people find their identity and source of self-worth in email and social media. I have seen people whose days are run completely by email. Eventually, it consumes and runs them.

The same goes for social media. People find their worth and value based on likes, followers, and whether or not people interact with them online. Let me be brutally honest with you. Email is a way to communicate. It doesn't run you, but you've allowed it to. Email or communication is on your terms and in your time. Your bank isn't open 24 hours a day. Your stores aren't open 24 hours a day. Why are you? Because you haven't told the world your boundaries. As Tim described, add an autoresponder to your email about the 12 p.m. and 4 p.m. response times. Do the same with your social media. You are only allowed to check in at noon and 4.

You have to realize that social media is a tool to sell things and get the word out. Spending a large part of your time crafting a post to let people know about the great thing you are eating or how your cat is doing is a time bandit that you are feeding when you should be growing your business.

Bottom line, email and social media are tools to get your business done. They are not an identity. If you are wondering whether or not you have an issue, I would challenge you to start with a 12 p.m. and 4 p.m. check-in. Then put it away. If you feel like you're going through withdrawals and getting cranky, it's probably a sign that your worth and value are dependent on being online.

By implementing this discipline, you will notice an increase in productivity. Your self-worth will start to rise. You'll see an increase in confidence because you are in control of your day. More importantly, everyone else's negligence or fire drills suddenly are no longer your problem to respond to immediately. If you have customers or clients who demand you every hour of every day, then get new clients. Email and social media are hamster wheels. They make you super busy without producing much. Get off the wheel.

Email and social media don't run you or your day. You do. The question becomes, what will you do with all the hundreds of hours you now have?

Have an amazing day!

13

Time Mastery vs. Time Management

TIME MASTERY VS. TIME MANAGEMENT

T he life of an entrepreneur is one of the greatest adventures imaginable. It is filled with highs and lows and venturing into the unknown. You take risks and pioneer through brand new, uncharted territories.

As I've travelled the last thirty years of my journey into entrepreneurship, I've realized something that should be obvious to everyone: The longer I live, the less time I have to accomplish all of my dreams. This haunts me every day. It is a sobering reminder of the fragility of our stint on earth.

Most people avoid thinking about this topic. But I believe it is one of the greatest motivators to get things done. The more I think about what my tombstone will say, the more laser-focused on my time mastery I become.

When it comes to your time, you have only a few options. You can spend it, you can waste it, or you can invest it.

Time management takes a passive view. You look at the time that you have in the day and take steps to minimize waste. But in my opinion, this is a half measure. Simply minimizing waste is not good enough. When you get to the end of your life, will you think about how efficiently you were able to get work done? Of course not.

Time mastery is a more aggressive approach. It is a radical mindset. Instead of thinking of ways to reduce wasted time, mastery focuses on how you can invest your time to dramatically increase your work rate and reduce the amount of hours spent working. What can you do to minimize waste and cut your workday in half?

Time management shows that time is running you. Time mastery shows that you run your time. One of the greatest disciplines of a successful entrepreneur is continually improving his or her mastery of time.

Whoever controls your calendar controls you.

BOB SHANK

Think about which 20% of your efforts, products, or work produce 80% of your revenue? What if you trimmed all the dead weight? If you focused more on the 20%, what would your life look like? How would you feel about your day? How much of your time is spent doing what you actually want.

Those who are willing to invest in time mastery force themselves to work the same amount in a shorter time frame. They are willing to do whatever it takes to free up more hours with family and valuable relationships. The goal is to hack your time. Instead of working an eight-hour day, give yourself three hours to do the same work. You will guard your alerts, interruptions, and distractions. You will learn that most of your time has been wasted or stolen by time bandits.

You will not get back the minutes of today. So invest them.

Have an amazing day.

121

Focused

Work

FOCUSED WORK

I recently heard an interview where a successful entrepreneur was asked: What is your key to success? His answer: the ability to focus.

Now, focus has different meanings for different people. For some, it means paying attention. For others, it's the ability to work without distraction or interference.

The focus I am talking about is the ability to focus in your work and craft. Entrepreneurs can suffer from "shiny object syndrome," where they sign up for everything they see and take on every new project that comes their way. These shiny objects consist of courses, business opportunities, investments, and builds.

Strategic and smart entrepreneurs have the ability and strength to exercise restraint. Shiny object syndrome is usually rooted in the fear of missing out on a project or opportunity that will help you become more successful.

Now, when it comes to your craft, whether it be writing, forecasting budgets, producing music, or scripting an email campaign, the idea of focused work can radically improve your outcomes.

In Cal Newport's book, *Deep Work*, he describes the psychological benefits of being able to focus during a very concentrated amount of time. He explains how the human brain works best during a three- to four-hour intense focused time period. I personally have gained massive productivity in developing the discipline to have focused work in the first four to five hours of the day. By developing this discipline, you will not only create more work, but you will create better work and results.

Challenge: In a previous chapter, I explained the discipline of being an early riser, which pays enormous dividends in creativity. I want to challenge you to take the first four to five hours a day and use them for uninterrupted and undistracted work. I would also suggest not checking your email or social media until midday and the afternoon. Twice a day is all that is needed for email and social media.

This kind of focused living is disciplined, defined, and measurable. The hidden value is that focused work is on your terms. Focused work provides safety and comfort. Great vision, dreams, and strategy can be birthed from a safe environment.

Imagine time by yourself dreaming, writing, and discovering more about yourself and your craft. The discipline of focused work is one of the greatest self-care actions you can develop.

Take today and become super intentional about carving out and protecting these times with yourself.

Have an amazing day.

———————————————

15

Self-Imposed Deadlines

SELF-IMPOSED DEADLINES

I have met and worked with countless entrepreneurs who struggle with launching, executing, and getting things done. They spend their days thinking about all the things they want to do, but at the end of the day, their only accomplishment is a journal filled with ideas. These journals and planners end up just being dream catchers that never see the light of day.

Most entrepreneurs are on a solo mission to bring ideas to life. We usually don't have other entrepreneurs around telling us if our strategies are right or wrong. Even if you have a team working with you, it's not their job to hold you accountable.

As an entrepreneur, it can be easy to fall into the trap of operating in this kind of vacuum. What happens is you end up judging yourself by intentions. This is usually the case when it comes to dreaming and thinking about strategies or initiatives. Procrastination can definitely play a role in self-sabotage as a creative.

This subtle trap can catch up to you and sabotage your productivity. Wise leaders always surround themselves with advisors—a coach or mentor to whom they can be accountable. There are reasons why this is so important.

Consider these realities:

1. Entrepreneurs usually judge themselves by their intentions, not by their outcomes.

2. Entrepreneurs tend to rationalize and make excuses for why their dreams don't become reality.

3. Entrepreneurs don't have a self-imposed system of getting ideas launched.

Remember when you were in school and had to cram for a test the night before? It was like there was a gun pointed at your head. You had to get it done in record time. The crazy thing is that it worked and you scored well.

Action: Take a moment to ask yourself the following questions:

1. Is my daily self-talk mostly about ideas, grandiose dreams, and visions of "what I will do soon"?

2. Does each New Year's Eve find you coming up short on the dreams and goals you had set for yourself or your business?

3. Have you settled for the status quo, no longer dreaming of launching new ideas? Are you comfortable and staying away from anything fresh or innovative?

If you choose to create radical self-imposed deadlines, you will dramatically increase your chances of making more revenue, creating more momentum, and having more time and money to make an impact around you. But this doesn't happen by luck, hope, or wishing. It is planned and enforced by you and for you.

Implement the habit of self-imposed deadlines. Make them radical and force yourself to do things in a third of the time you normally would. You will increase your output, create more time, and generate revenue sooner.

Most leaders say, "Ready, aim, aim, aim, aim." Very few fire. Set your launch days in stone and stick to them.

Lazy hands make for poverty, but diligent hands bring wealth.
- PROVERBS 10:4 NIV

Have an amazing day!

16

Get Naked in

Relationships

GET NAKED IN RELATIONSHIPS

Communication is one of the key ingredients to growing intimacy and trust in all relationships. Entrepreneurs can default to thinking that this only means personal relationships, when in fact it applies to business relationships too.

A key discipline an entrepreneur can develop is getting naked, and there are a few crucial areas where this applies to business relationships.

Contracts: Entrepreneurs who discipline themselves early in a business negotiation mitigate the risk of emotional fallout later. If you are willing to create a deal point memo and have a discussion about all the potential blind spots, then you will safeguard your relationships, make more money, and build more clients. You create safety, trust, and relational equity sooner.

Rogue Waves: Most entrepreneurs I have encountered have no idea how to handle conflict, surprises, or unexpected roadblocks. It could be an order gone wrong, a damaged item, a product return, an unhappy customer, or an upset client.

Even more challenging is how to handle buying out a partner, dismantling a client under contract, or having to renegotiate a contract already underway. All of these scenarios include two key factors: uncertainty and the fear of the unknown. And fear can absolutely paralyze an entrepreneur.

But the key to defusing the bomb is surprising—the key is getting naked. Entrepreneurs are creative, and they will actualize what might happen. We build the issue up more than what it actually is. The key is to drop the fig leaf and get naked as soon as possible.

So what do I mean by getting naked? Getting naked means meeting in person or meeting over the phone to share your heart, including sharing your desires to find a win-win solution.

Stop communicating through text and email. It's disrespectful and shows you are a coward playing small. Real leaders catch a flight to meet, drive hours to talk face-to-face, or call to discuss the issues. You should be as reasonable as possible regardless of what your contract says. Give more than you should. How you handle conflict says a lot to others how about your integrity. Your integrity has a ripple effect forever, especially if it is online. Even more, your integrity is relational equity. It's one of the greatest assets to invest in.

Challenge: Where in life are you playing small in your communication? Who haven't you been honest and naked with? Is there a relationship nagging or tugging at your gut that might qualify as unfinished business? Would getting naked possibly take your relational equity to a new level? Do you need to forgive anyone? Is there someone you need to meet with or apologize to?

Getting naked in relationships is one of the greatest disciplines you can develop to become successful. This process becomes easier each time you do it, but you will find the peace and freedom that comes on the other side is priceless. Be one of the few who step into being real with themselves and others.

Have an amazing day.

17

Negotiating: Lead with a Feather but Have a Hammer in Your Back Pocket

NEGOTIATING: LEAD WITH A FEATHER BUT HAVE A HAMMER IN YOUR BACK POCKET

The entrepreneurial culture often feels like it's dog-eat-dog. Everyone is out for themselves, scrambling to do whatever it takes to get what they want. But few people realize that how we go about getting what we want has a massive ripple effect on our relationships with clients, employees, and family.

How you do anything speaks volumes about who you are as a person. Whether it's parenting, business, art, or driving a car, it's the how that communicates everything.

Negotiating is no different. Negotiating is a skill that must be mastered through practice. How you negotiate not only determines whether or not you will succeed, but it also says something about you. I have learned that successful negotiating requires two important tools: a and a .

Let's say you're heading into a very confrontational meeting, negotiation, or phone call. The person or organization you're about to interact with has wronged you in some way. You have every right to go in with guns blazing to get what you want.

However, the feather approach prefers to lead the conversation with questions to gain understanding. You ask every question in a tone that is unoffending and gentle. You manage your speech. You conduct your negotiations with the feather approach. Stephen Covey wrote that one of the best habits to develop is to first seek to understand before being understood. This concept is central to negotiation with a feather.

While you're in this discussion, it will take every bit of strength and discipline to keep the hammer in your pocket and only use it if and when necessary. Think about it: How many people do you know who react to situations with a sledgehammer and bulldozer when they could have used a feather and hammer and received better outcomes and results?

I have personally witnessed a business owner implode because of the way he talked to other people and handled his negotiations. Knee-jerk reactions to situations or accusations so often occur when we want to exact justice. If someone accuses our business, an employee, our spouse, or even our kids, we can immediately take things personally. This is a natural response. But I want to encourage you to pause and consider a discipline that can radically impact your negotiations and selling.

Remember, you are selling every day, whether you realize it or not. This is where most entrepreneurs and leaders get blindsided. How you conduct yourself creates a ripple effect of your integrity for life. I have listened to men lean on the sword of their integrity only to forfeit future opportunity by committing relational suicide. It's never worth it.

I would ask you to evaluate your heart and ask yourself some hard questions: Do I get offended easily? Am I always cynical? Do I always feel people are out to get me? Do I find myself sabotaging every relationship, both personal and business, out of a lack of trust? Do I operate as a victim whenever I'm in negotiations? Am I willing to be reasonable? Do I ever strive and work hard to find a win-win? Do I ever consider my words and actions and how they will affect my integrity and reputation?

A helpful filter: Approach your negotiations with a feather. Lead the conversation with love, kindness, patience, and grace even if you've been wronged. Speak the truth in love in a tone that is nearly a whisper. If the other party is being unreasonable and overstepping appropriate conduct, pull out the hammer and enforce boundaries that are on your terms. But communicate them in love. You can still say you're hurt, wronged, or disappointed without causing damage.

The ripple effect of your integrity has an everlasting impact on the lives around you. Make it a discipline to pause and take inventory of your approach, your feelings, and your response. It can make or break the deal.

Have an amazing day!

18

The Power of Over-

Communication

THE POWER OF OVER-COMMUNICATION

They say the most important thing in marriage is communication. Communication shows respect for the other party. In my experiences, there are two specific components to communication: the "how" and the "what." Maintaining healthy relationships of all types— whether in marriage, business, or with clients—requires a high level of respect and conduct.

Even more important than what you communicate is how you communicate. This speaks volumes. Your tone and posture show a great deal about your heart, your intentions as a person, and the way you are wired. It also reveals if you are a safe person who can be trusted. Each time you violate, overstep, or act inappropriately, you take a "withdrawal" from the relational equity you have invested in people.

What you communicate, on the other hand, reveals your nature. I have seen people who are great at delivering a message, but they miss the mark on the content because they never allow themselves to become vulnerable. If you don't communicate your weaknesses and vulnerabilities, if you're not transparent with people, there will never be any growth or equity built. Think of relationships you may have had in the past that stagnated. You probably never talked about anything deeper than the weather, your job, and the surface stuff of life.

A lot of people might see this type of vulnerability as uncomfortable or maybe as "too much information." But I beg to differ. In my experience, over-communicating has never created a disadvantage. Successful entrepreneurs over-communicate with their spouses, their kids, and their customers. Remember, there is no downside to over-communicating. It shows that you care and value transparency.

So why don't we over-communicate? Possibly fear of rejection or being perceived as silly or too sensitive or weak. But I'm here to tell you that during our over thirty years of business, over-communicating has been one of our company's greatest assets. The more we communicate, the more equity and trust we build with others.

Personally, I'd rather deal with embarrassment than be misunderstood. I'd rather cope with being called silly or sensitive than make business decisions based on false assumptions or misinformation.

And by the way, I've never had a client, my wife, or a customer say that I communicate too much.

Challenge: Do you find that you're fearful of saying how you really feel about things because you're afraid of the potential fallout? Do you curb what you say because you're worried about how people will respond? If you were to communicate more of who you really are, what would that look like? Is it possible to be genuine and transparent without being inappropriate or off-putting? What is one area or person you could be more real with today?

Living with failure that occurs as a result of being real far outweighs the regret of not living transparently and honestly. Healthy relationships are always worthwhile because the more you share, the more people will open up. We all want to be known. And when we share what's inside, bringing secret things into the light, our isolation ends and the opportunity to be known as we truly are begins in our businesses and relationships.

Note: Most people won't receive this idea with open arms—guaranteed. But some will. So invest your heart wisely with people who will receive it with gentleness and love, not with those who will throw it to the ground and stomp on it. If you are willing to take the risk, deep growth and success as an entrepreneur will be your reward.

Have an amazing day.

19

Pull the Weeds in Relationships

PULL THE WEEDS IN RELATIONSHIPS

Without a doubt, relationships are one of the greatest assets in your life. You are exposed to many different types of relationships each day: family, coworkers, clients/customers, and friends. And every day, you have opportunities to grow and stretch these relationships. However, sometimes, certain relationships go sideways and conflict strikes. What do you do when this occurs?

You pull the weeds—as fast as possible.

In this life there will be relational trouble, those rogue waves we talked about earlier. They are absolutely guaranteed. It could be a client, employee, vendor, or family member. Typically, leaders retreat to a non-confrontational stance because they don't want to deal with these kinds of stressful relational dynamics. This is usually because they don't have the skills to dismantle these challenging situations. Confronting people is tough. Confronting people quickly is even tougher.

Nevertheless, it is crucial to realize that the longer you allow a situation to fester, the more it will spread and infect other areas your life, creativity, and performance. Think with me of the effect of a splinter. It's just a small sliver of wood, but it can produce a lot of pain and discomfort. If you pull it out right away, the pain greatly diminishes, and your body begins to heal and can recover quite quickly. But if you leave it in, it could fester and become infected.

How many of you have houses in your neighborhood where the yards have been completely neglected? The owners have let the weeds run wild, and what little grass there is hasn't been mowed or maintained. Your relationships can get like that yard if you don't pull the weeds quickly. Without this kind of maintenance, your interpersonal life can become overwhelmed by conflict and tension. Here are a few tips that you can use to develop this discipline of pulling the weeds:

1. **Ask yourself** if you're willing to let go of your pride and have the tough talk so everyone can find release and freedom as soon as possible. Staying in limbo typically causes an unnecessary standoff. Humble yourself, take the higher road, and avoid the drama.

2. **Be willing** to overlook an offense. You will probably not remember a small offense a few years from now. Is it worth putting so much time and energy into prolonging the issue?

3. **Respond**; don't react. How you handle conflict is paramount when it comes to your integrity with your family, business, and friends. Use these moments in life to learn about yourself and respond in a patient and kind manner.

4. **Freedom** is what you're after—the end goal. Work hard to not base your decisions on money you're owed. If someone has offended you, you prolong the issues by nickel-and-diming. What are you willing to let go of to gain freedom? Is holding onto a grudge really going to pay off? Holding onto resentment is a splinter in your heart that will become infected. It will rule you if you don't pull it out. You will gain freedom by letting go.

5. **Pulling the weeds** is a discipline that will pay massive dividends for you if used quickly. The sooner you do this, the sooner you will be able to move forward with a clear heart and a clean conscience.

Life is too short to waste time with people who cause problems. The wisest entrepreneurs I know are those with the ability to have tough conversations quickly.

How badly do you want freedom? How nice would it be to get rid of the weeds that preoccupy your mind? What would you do with all that new soil? Water the great relationships you have, learn from the ones that went sideways, and build healthy boundaries for the future.

Have an amazing day!

20

Conquering Life's Rogue Waves

CONQUERING LIFE'S ROGUE WAVES

When people first set out to go into business, they start with grand ideas and huge dreams. I totally believe that great things happen as a result of passion and drive. But what most new entrepreneurs never consider is that they are absolutely guaranteed to encounter a litany of trouble, chaos, and surprises on the voyage ahead.

Let me paint the picture for you. Imagine a ship in a harbor. This ship is your company and life. You are not just the captain of the ship or the engineer in the engine room: you own a fleet of ships around the world.

Now, while you are in port, your ship is sitting still. Everything looks pretty. Everyone is boarding and enjoying all of the amenities it offers. Most entrepreneurs build life based on this scenario. They develop a life and company that is predictable and controllable but miss out on the original purpose of the ship: to be at sea.

Entrepreneurs look at their beautiful brand and only imagine taking their ship out to sea over smooth waters. They rarely fantasize about handling, both personally or professionally, what I call "rogue waves."

Rogue waves are circumstances and issues in life that surprise you. They are like a tsunami that comes out of nowhere and creates chaos. Rogue waves are simply a part of the life you signed up for. The question is, will you be someone who reacts to them or someone who prepares for them?

Life and business are unpredictable. Rest assured that you will encounter rogue waves. Even still, business owners worry themselves to death and become paralyzed about possible conflict and what lies ahead on the open seas. Living this way isn't healthy. As a leader and owner of your business, you set the tone, pace, and confidence for your team.

Here are some ways you can discipline your mind and approach to conflict.

If you are a business owner and entrepreneur, you need to get an accurate outlook on yourself and your identity. You are a risk taker and a pioneer. Those two words welcome conflict, so why are you wearing yourself out trying to always keep things peaceful?

Rogue waves come in many different forms. It could be something as dramatic as an employee suing you. Your next rogue wave could be a customer getting super upset because a shipping company damaged their items. Maybe it's a health issue or one of your kids rebelling. Your business partner could betray you or someone might steal from you. Your brand could get raked over the coals in the press or trashed by haters and trolls online. You get the idea. Let me share a discipline I use to help stay buoyant.

Tip: A healthy discipline is to sit down and take inventory of your triggers and feelings. You will learn that what triggers you will often be rooted in one of two things: fear or shame.

Shame says your value is based on what you do and the quality of your work. If you are truly a good person, then you should be getting praise, connections, love, money, and security.

As a Type-A driven entrepreneur, this is most likely how you define yourself—by your performance. But this is a slippery slope and a massive blind spot. Why? Because what happens when a rogue wave inevitably comes and slashes your performance? Your self-worth immediately goes down the drain.

If you are proactive and use the discipline of sitting down to honestly identify your triggers and feelings, you can prepare for this. When the next rogue wave hits, take the opportunity to dig into your feelings and try to identify the source of your shame. Lean into it and search it. When you discover the source, write it down, examine it thoroughly, and pray about it.

Here's my thought process when I feel shame start to creep in to sabotage me. I remember that my identity and how I feel about myself isn't determined by my performance or anything outside of me. My self-worth is found in whom I belong to: Jesus Christ. My relationship with God through His Son Jesus is the only force in the universe that is unchanging and totally reliable.

God's love for you cannot be shaken, denied, or removed. His love is in constant pursuit of your heart every day. Do you feel tired of managing the stress, outcomes, and responsibilities? Discipline your mind to hold onto the truth that you don't own your business. It's owned by God. You get to use it. You get to manage it.

Oh, and by the way, you already have wealth and abundance because God gave you the power and the ability to create wealth. Everything changes once you surrender your will and put your trust in Him. He owns it all. Therefore, have joy and peace that He works together all things on your behalf and has nothing but good in store for you if you earnestly seek Him.

My business went into hyper-drive the moment I stopped acting like I had control of the helm. I don't. God does. Your life, your ship, and the course He has planned for you will be beyond anything you could possibly imagine.

Your inner peace and joy as a business owner is based on your source of security. If your source of security is your business, yourself, or the circumstances of life that you happen to be in at this moment, then all you will manage is chaos. You will constantly be let down. If your source is in the ultimate creative Entrepreneur, you will be able to navigate life with assurance.

Discipline your thinking to see God as your director and yourself as the producer. Ultimately, He created you, your talent, and your business.

The key is to not make Him a silent partner.

Have an amazing day.

———————————————

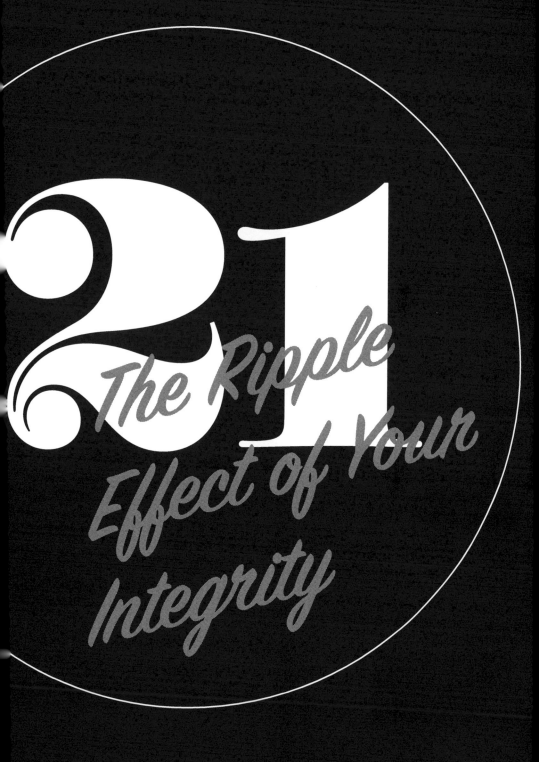

21

The Ripple Effect of Your Integrity

THE RIPPLE EFFECT OF YOUR INTEGRITY

R ecently, I met with one of my coaching students and discussed some challenging decisions he needed to make. Like most entrepreneurs, he was focused on how he could win the negotiation and benefit his own life and career. I agreed that the negotiations were important. But I also stressed how important it was to consider how our words and actions have ripple effects.

This idea—that our actions and words stretch far beyond our conversations and interactions—is one of the most powerful filters I use in decision-making.

It's the discipline of remembering the ripple effect of your integrity.

You see, most leaders can forecast and implement strategies that produce incredible outcomes. However, even the best leaders are vulnerable to this common blind spot: They no longer remember or recognize that words and actions can dismantle years of hard work, money, and effort if integrity is not maintained.

How can you make this a healthy discipline? Here are a few steps to keep you in check and to protect you from yourself:

1. When it comes to negotiations and discussions, how you speak is just as important as what you are trying to communicate. I have seen young leaders emotionally vomit during a meeting or conference call due to insecurities and the lack the self-awareness, which is needed to navigate the discussions. Fear gets the best of them, and they get emotional.

2. Your words echo your heart. If you don't know what to say, don't say anything. Silence is the greatest negotiator.

3. If you are offended easily, get triggered easily, or are guarded in relationships, there is a strong possibility you are operating out of a wound from your past or childhood. If fear runs your dialogue, the people in the room will detect it in a heartbeat. This issue alone can ruin and dismantle years of relational equity. Operating from a wound will tag you as "unsafe" and "out of bounds" to people who might want to work with you. Situations or circumstances that are highly stressful bring out the best or worst in people. Companies, customers, and organizations want to know that they can deal with solid, reliable people who don't go sideways. If you were to analyze yourself, would you say you respond or react to challenges? Do you become easily agitated and triggered? Do you have the emotional grit to operate in peace regardless of the hurricane around you?

4. What is said online stays online. I've seen more brands and reputations ruined by saying the wrong thing online. There is no Command-Z online. You can't hit the "Undo" button. Once it's out there, it's there for good. When I coach and consult brands, I drive home the importance of how your online history creates your integrity. For example, my YouTube channel, blogs, and my previous relationships ALL form the integrity of my businesses and personal life. Why is this important? Because your past and present are your business card. I have had numerous students, clients, and customers comb through the years of content that has been created to validate and learn about our story. So don't take this lightly and unwisely think that what you post is just for fun and games. The fact is, if you're trying to build your own brand, people will go through the highlight reel of your online presence and relationships to vet your integrity.

My friend, you can make investments in building financial equity. You can invest in spiritual growth to create spiritual equity. But the greatest lack of investment I see in leaders is the discipline to create relational equity.

May today mark the beginning of intentionally focusing on what you say and how you say it. May the time you spend with people put wind in their sails.

A good name is to be more desired than great wealth, favor is better than silver and gold. - **PROVERBS 22:1 NASB**

Have an amazing day!

22
Exercise Your Mind and Body

EXERCISE YOUR MIND AND BODY

One of the most overlooked aspects of leadership is physical wellness. As a leader, your life is running at a speed and pace that isn't typical for the rest of the world. You spend your day handling your responsibilities and challenges while fighting to make time for yourself. However, a common discipline that is often ignored is physical and mental exercise.

Even if you are someone who sits in a chair all day at a computer, it is essential to be physically active to perform at your best. Physical exercise will transform your work and performance.

Here are five disciplines that I feel will radically help you in your performance as a leader:

1. **Be consistent:** As we learned in the "early bird gets the worm" chapter, plan the evening before by preparing for an early morning. Have your morning routine start at least two hours before your normal day. Start with quiet time, prayer, and devotions. Listen and be still. Write in your journal. Then move into focused work. This could be writing and/or planning. The reason for early mornings is due to the fact that your mind is at its sharpest after a good night's sleep.

2. **Be active:** Once you've wrapped up your morning quiet time and focused work, move into exercise. Your mind will need the rest. Your exercise can include various forms, depending on what you enjoy. If you're just beginning, take your phone and use the health app to track your steps. Go for a walk and try to get in at least 10,000 steps. Even if you are walking in the dark before sunup, I can guarantee this: You will experience some of the most sacred times with yourself. Important note: If you are walking, running, or on a treadmill, be sure to listen to an audiobook, podcast, or some life-giving content. This is about filling your cup, which leads me to my next point.

3. **Be a reader:** Leaders are readers. One discipline I've learned from successful entrepreneurs is the art of reading. They are in a constant state of gathering and digesting wisdom through books. This can be done via audiobook or reading chapters from books that pertain most to your life and situation. I don't waste time reading what I don't need.

4. **Be sacrificial:** Intermittently fasting is a discipline that has radically changed my life. Most people fast for 16 hours a day and then eat during an eight-hour window. However, I choose to fast for 18-21 hours each day and give myself an eating window between 5-8 p.m. This discipline pays massive dividends. Your body isn't interrupted from healing all day and night. You save a ton of money. The preoccupation of where and what to eat are eliminated from your mental preoccupations throughout the day. You will actually gain additional hours of production without having your day run by food. For beginners, start with eating between 1 p.m. and 10 p.m. daily. Your metabolism, your organs, and body will heal as well as perform at a level you couldn't imagine. Your human growth hormone increases and your body repairs itself quickly. There are numerous books and resources on intermittent fasting. Study this discipline. You'll be amazed at what is possible.

5. **Be disciplined:** Physical discipline might be one of the absolute best things you can do for your life. You might hate it or you might love it. For most, exercise is foreign. Let me tell you, if you can master the discipline of exercise, you will place yourself in the very small percentage of the world of leaders. I recently was able to motivate and incentivize our teenage son to go to the gym with me four days a week for weight training. How did I do this? I told him that he can have a full pint of ice cream on Sundays on his cheat day. If he misses any workouts, he doesn't get the pint. We are approaching the one-year mark of him going every week for four days. This has transformed his mental state and his physical appearance. His mom is in a constant state of rolling her eyes because he's always flexing and saying, "Feel these guns," as he kisses each bicep. Working out allows us to hang out together, but more importantly, he has learned that he is capable of overcoming himself. He pushes himself to go beyond what he thought was possible. Just getting to the gym is actually 80 percent of the overcoming. I truly believe that if every kid learned this discipline, it would transform our culture.

The person whose morning routine begins with soul care, mind care, and physical care can go into the day focused, balanced, filled, and confident. You will literally be facing the day from a position of strength.

You don't have to choose only one form of exercise. There are dozens of different types. I have done yoga, powerlifting, running, and strength training. If you're a beginner, start with quick-paced walking, 10,000 steps at least four days a week. For intermediate, you could start jogging four miles a day or going to the gym for circuit training. A great resource for both men and women is bodybuilding.com, but my favorite has been Man 2.0, Engineering the Alpha, by John Romaniello and Adam Bornstein. This book is the most comprehensive resource on health and wellness I have found in over thirty years (just know that there are a lot of F-bombs in the material). These principles and strategies changed my life. Guys, you will have the ability to reset your hormones, modify your insulin resistance, increase your testosterone, and increase strength.

Why I implement physical exercise: One of the most important reasons for taking care of myself physically is for a greater quality of life and for longevity. I asked my mentors why they still exercise and read daily at 70+ years old, and their answers surprised me a little: They said it was so they would have more time to bear more fruit. Obviously, in order to bear fruit, you have to be alive. Plus, the older you get, the wiser you are; you're connected to more influential people, so you have more tools at your disposal. Why would you want life to end short or early? On top of all of that, exercise acts as a natural antidepressant and releases hormones that balance your mental health, while reading and gathering wisdom sharpens the mind and stretches you into a greater human.

Your body is important, but your mind is even more crucial because it will increase in strength and power while your body wears out. Therefore, sharpen and strengthen your mind. First Timothy 4:8 says, "For physical training is of some value, but godliness has value for all things, holding promise for both the present life and the life to come" (NIV). Sharpen the saw of your mind with wisdom, and you'll be in a league beyond anyone else in your marriage, parenting, career, and relationships. Wisdom is more precious than silver or gold.

You are what you eat, physically and mentally. Have an amazing day!

23

Your #1 Client: Your Spouse

YOUR #1 CLIENT: YOUR SPOUSE

When you get out of bed in the morning, you probably have a laundry list of action items you want to get done. I understand this perfectly. This is how the mind of an entrepreneur works. For the first ten years of my career, I got up every morning and charged diligently through my list of daily tasks.

I did this because I believed with all my heart that my main goal should be to earn and provide for my wife and kids. In turn, she (and they) would love me. The funny thing was, I had it backwards.

What she really wanted was for me to have fun in my craft and for us to spend quality time together building memories. Instead, I was putting all of my energy into trying to perform and please her. I was completely worn out because I had the right drive, but I was aiming at the wrong target.

As an entrepreneur, your life is probably packed with meetings, relationships, collaborations, and initiatives. But no matter how much prestige, fame, wealth, or influence they produce, those things cannot come at the expense of your marriage.

The most effective entrepreneurs I have ever met and interviewed all have this one thing in common: They have made their spouse their number one client.

Here's how my wife Chantel and I have accomplished this. For the last eighteen years, we've invested one night each week on a date night. During this night, we are intentional about taking inventory on our marriage, careers, and parenting. We ask what we like least about the current season we're in and what we want more of.

Here's the bottom line: Your marriage is the bedrock—the foundation of everything else in your day and life. When you make him or her your number one client and priority, you will see the dynamic of your marriage and family change around you.

Tip: If you have trouble connecting with your spouse and things are challenging, make weekly dates to have intentional time with each other. During these times, become a professional listener like you are with your most valued clients. Find out their greatest needs and dreams the same way you would with your clients. Then create plans and strategies to underwrite and support their dreams. This is your chance to put yourself aside and serve the heart of your spouse.

If you don't take care of your spouse and children, someone else will.

Action: Answer this question, "If my best friend were to ask my spouse to grade me on our marriage, what would my report card be?" I firmly believe that as entrepreneurs, we have no business trying to change the lives of the people in our company and in the world through our products if we haven't first served our number one priority: our spouse and children.

Your spouse has the ability to reveal your blind spots and hidden value better than anyone else. Marriage is a blessing, not a burden. It should be a haven and provide stability and freedom. Your spouse is your number one client. Would he or she agree?

Today, begin putting one drop at a time into the bucket of your spouse's emotional account. It's an investment that will pay the most return and dividends.

21

Investing in "Best Days" with Your Kids

INVESTING IN "BEST DAYS"
WITH YOUR KIDS

Have you ever found yourself working in the office and feeling overwhelmed with responsibilities and the pressure to leave on time to make your child's sporting event that evening? What about the daily self-doubt that says you aren't giving your kids the time and memories they deserve? I've been there and can totally relate to these thoughts.

I want to share some insight into a useful discipline that I learned from successful entrepreneurs on how they go about battling this self-doubt.

Before you read any further, I want to issue this caveat: What I'm about to say is not meant to be a substitution for developing a healthy work/life balance. Part of being an entrepreneur is learning when it's time to end the workday and focus on your spouse and kids.

With that being said, finding that balance is not at all easy. If you do have kids, then you know what it's like to be torn between how much time we give career and how much time we give family. This tension isn't going to go away even when your kids are adults. So let's shed light on a discipline you can use to invest in quality time with your kids.

The term "best day" describes a day that you have carved out of the schedule in order to be 100 percent focused on your child. There are rules: no movies and no TV or devices. Other than that, they get to pick what happens from sunup to sundown. They get to go anywhere they want and eat anything they want, as much as they want.

Basically, this is a yes day. While they are little, it could mean playing miniature golf, eating ice cream, laser tag, and going to their favorite restaurant for lunch. When they're older, it could be river rafting, horseback riding, or zip lining. They might want to visit castles in England. No matter what it is, your answer is "yes." You might have to plan and save. But in the meantime, you can stay local with no holds barred.

Examples: When I asked my seven-year-old daughter where she wanted to go, it was the Pancake House for breakfast, then Disneyland, and then In-n-Out Burger for dinner. At fourteen, she requested flying to Vegas to stay in a fancy hotel and to see Michael Jackson's "One" by Cirque du Soleil followed by lunch and round of golf at Top Golf.

It was epic. It's a memory neither one of us will ever forget. She held my hand as we walked around. It was focused dad-and-daughter time without any interruptions. As we sat at the burger joint she chose for lunch and ate ice cream, she shared the ups and downs of her world with school, friends, and dreams. It was a trip for the books.

Then there was the time with Li'l Noah who, after seeing the movies *Home Alone* and *Elf*, wanted to fly first class to New York, stay at the Plaza Hotel, and have pizza and ice cream. We visited the American Museum of Natural History and walked down just about every street in Manhattan. This was the week before Christmas and the city looked like a movie set. It began snowing as we walked back from the Lego® store with his new build and settled down for the last night.

As an entrepreneur, one of the greatest disciplines you can implement is becoming the underwriter of your family's dreams. Sure, we can build companies and brands that impact our employees and customers. But the most important clients in our lives are our spouse and kids. Make them the example and your greatest client. You won't get these years back. This is the last year they will be this age.

Think about it: You won't be on your deathbed wishing you would have spent more time at the office.

Action: The next time you're with your kids at a meal, just ask them, "If you could go anywhere for one day, do anything you want, and eat whatever you want, where would you want to go, and what would you want to do?" Then, once you hear their answer, put a date on the calendar and start planning. The greatest part of this will be the anticipation they feel as they look forward to it.

Tip: I would encourage you to tell your team and clients not to contact you at all on this day. Go dark as much as you can. Your goal is to be present, off the grid, focusing on your child completely. They'll know if you've made this a priority based on the interruptions, texts, and phone calls. Also, take tons of pictures and post them online. Gloat over the memories you built. Celebrate them.

Finally, let's flip this around. When was the last time you invested time in the kid in you? I make it an aim to spend about two to three hours Saturday and Sunday mornings before the family is up to drive to my favorite coffee spot, sit on the beach cliffs, and fill my cup through time with God and prayer. It realigns my priorities and goals. It lets me play in my mental sandbox to dream the next dream. Take the kid in you out. When was the last time he or she heard from you?

25

Yearly Retreat:
Self & Business
Inventory

YEARLY RETREAT: SELF & BUSINESS INVENTORY

The journey of being an entrepreneur includes so many responsibilities that you can quickly lose yourself in the minutiae. There's so much going on in every department of your business that it can feel like you're the only one who can do it all. This is why most entrepreneurs fear taking a break because they feel that things will fall apart without them managing every aspect of the business.

However, self-care and inventory are key to the overall health and wellness of you, your family, team, and initiatives. If you continue to run on empty, it's like trying to pour from an empty glass. Eventually you'll have nothing left.

Another essential discipline that will help you establish a healthy perspective is to take time each year to assess and measure each area of your life and business. You should also take this assessment each quarter to establish a system of checks and balances.

Here are a few questions that can help reveal hidden value you aren't seeing and possible blind spots:

1.   On a scale of 1-10, how is my overall satisfaction with my health? What adjustments can I make to have this number go up 1-2 points?

2.   On a scale of 1-10, how is my overall satisfaction with my marriage? What adjustments can I make to have this number go up 1-2 points?

3.   On a scale of 1-10, how is my overall satisfaction with my friendships? What adjustments can I make to have this number go up 1-2 points?

4.   On a scale of 1-10, how is my overall satisfaction with my finances? What adjustments can I make to have this number go up 1-2 points? Do I base my identity on my financial well-being?

5. On a scale of 1-10, how is my overall satisfaction with my alone time and investing in myself? What adjustments can I make to have this number go up 1-2 points? (Consider planning weekly or quarterly dates to book yourself as a client.)

6. On a scale of 1-10, how is my overall satisfaction with my mental outlook (intellect)? What adjustments can I make to have this number go up 1-2 points? (Consider a new book, a course, or a mentorship. Also, who is speaking into your life and stretching you?)

Taking inventory on yourself as an entrepreneur will allow you to detect the potential blind spots and discover the hidden value you aren't seeing.

Have an amazing day.

26

Avoid the Comparison Trap

AVOID THE COMPARISON TRAP

Back when I was first venturing into the world of business and building my brand, there weren't as many media outlets as there are today. There were landlines, newspapers, radio, TV, newspapers, and direct mail—that was it. If you wanted to see what was going on in other people's lives, you had to read a newspaper, pick up the phone, or turn on the television.

Today, all of us have mobile phones in our pockets that keep us in touch with millions of people around the world. We even get notified instantly if a celebrity or one of our friends do or say anything.

This has led to us spending countless hours watching highlight reels of everyone around us. Consequently and inevitably, these highlight reels have become the new grid—the new paradigm—through which we view ourselves.

However, I have a stern warning for you: There is a trap waiting for you inside this new paradigm. If you don't possess discipline and a sober mindset, you are going to become its victim.

It's called the Comparison Trap.

Here's an illustration. When you take up a new hobby like playing guitar or becoming a musician, you take some lessons to get the basics down. But then you progress and learn more advanced techniques and play more difficult songs. Eventually, you try to test yourself and prove how good you are by imitating and playing cover songs.

It's the same way with building our companies and launching our dreams. We see someone doing what we want, and we imitate their efforts to get the hang of things. The trouble starts when we use other people's success and effort as a gauge for our own feelings of self-worth. If we see other people enjoying the success that we want but don't have, it makes us feel worthless and discouraged.

Listen: It takes guts and grit to give life to an idea, build it out, and create a new venture or business out of thin air. I commend you for dreaming, building, and launching. But I want to warn you right now that the Comparison Trap is a blind spot, and it is nearly guaranteed. You are not immune to its effect.

Once successful entrepreneurs prove to themselves that they have what it takes, they set their minds to becoming pioneers, and they never look back. The greatest leaders have the discipline to stay in their lane—to keep the blinders on rather than trying to see where other people are in the race. They maintain a laser-like focus on their calling and mission without looking to others for their self-worth.

Challenge: Take a quick inventory. When you see others in your field succeed, are you stoked for them or are you envious? When you are around others, do you need to be the one who is above everyone else? Do you find yourself apprehensive to share ideas and collaborate out of fear of being hurt or betrayed? Where are you with entrusting your heart to others?

Comparison can lead to resentment and envy, which will pollute the soul.

Solution: There is a common trait among successful, creative entrepreneurs that I've encountered. They know that their calling and life assignment isn't to be compared to anyone else's life. God made each one of us unique. There will not be anyone before you or after you who will fulfill your calling. If that's the case, why compare yourself to others? You have a story to tell and a life to live. Be you. Everyone else is taken.

Have an amazing day!

———————————

27

If It Doesn't Have Your Name on It, Get Rid of It ASAP

IF IT DOESN'T HAVE YOUR NAME ON IT, GET RID OF IT ASAP

In a previous chapter, I drove home the point that we have very limited time in this life. You've probably also realized that life is a blink and years pass quicker as we grow older.

One of the disciplines I have witnessed in successful entrepreneurs is the ability to "buy time" through delegating. Delegation is difficult for most people because they listen to the lie that they will lose control if they let go and let someone else do the work for them. If an entrepreneur refuses to delegate, he or she runs the risk of juggling too many plates. When too many plates are going at once, the entrepreneur feels very busy but isn't actually producing results or gaining any ground.

You can create more time for yourself by having someone else handle the responsibilities facing you. Below, I have compiled a few lists to consider that can help you scale your abilities without losing quality or excellence in your execution.

First, the easiest way to tell if you should delegate a task or responsibility is this: Simply ask yourself if someone else can do it. If the answer is yes, then you need to get out of that role ASAP. Just because you can do your own bookkeeping and clean your office doesn't mean you "should." You can buy that time back if you discharge those tasks to others.

Second, hire people who are smarter than you. This is something that a surprising amount of entrepreneurs avoid. They often feel threatened hiring people who are smarter than them or better than them at certain tasks. But that's the whole point! If you want to maintain the quality of your work, then you need to hire people who are as good or better than you are.

Third, if you can't hire, then recruit an intern who is smarter than you.

Begin paying them as you start to make revenue.

Fourth, when I hire, I make sure that I choose partners who don't require being disciplined or constantly managed and who produce world-class results.

Successful creative entrepreneurs know that it is critical to leverage other people's genius to raise the bar for everyone. If you as a leader want to grow to new heights, it requires lightening your load so you can focus on your own creativity to produce the greatest return and value.

Remember, if someone else can do what you're doing, get out and hire someone to do it.

Action: Make a list in your journal of the most time-sucking tasks and responsibilities that drain your batteries. Next, make a list of your responsibilities that are life-giving, that you would almost do for free because you love them so much. Now, how aggressive are you willing to get with yourself in delegating those tasks that take up too much of your time and wear you down?

Potential blind spot: If you delegate some responsibility and buy back four to six hours each day, the tendency will be to fill the newfound time with social media and miscellaneous fillers. But successful creatives fill that time with productive investments that yield greater results in half the time. You can now create incredible results in one third of the time. Then, take the remaining time to do self-care and spend time building memories with your family and friends.

Have an amazing day!

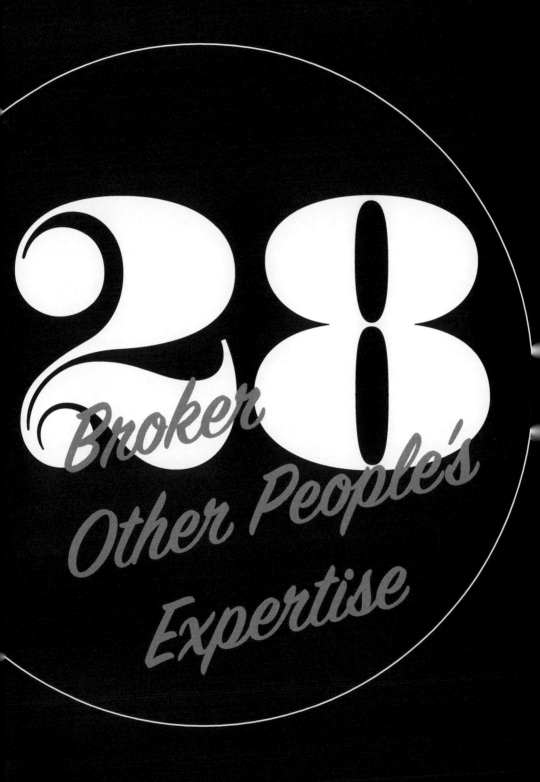

28

Broker
Other People's
Expertise

BROKER OTHER PEOPLE'S EXPERTISE

Entrepreneurs often operate like jugglers, spinning twenty-plus plates in the air every single day. I once coached a client whose "plates" included making, packaging, and shipping her product, as well as taking care of customer service. Her duties left little to no time for strategizing and planning for the future.

This kind of pedal-to-the-floor effort is a one-way ticket to burnout. But there is a way to prevent it. Even more exciting, there is a discipline and secret to getting it all done while actually doing less.

In *The E-Myth* by Michael Gerber, he explains the three versions of an entrepreneur. There's the person doing the craft, the person doing the managing, and the person growing the business. The reality is, you can only be two of these at a time. Like the woman I was coaching, she realized that she couldn't wear all the hats. Even more importantly, her business could not scale the way she was doing things.

One of the biggest and most exciting pleasures in my life is watching the lights turn on in the business and life of someone I'm coaching. I love it when those who have searched for gold actually find it. A major breakthrough occurs when I can help entrepreneurs find a system of brokering. Some might call this subcontracting or internship and those labels do apply. But I call it brokering.

When I started my business at sixteen, I was doing graphics, signs, and illustration. Greater success came when I was able to leverage the local sign shop for all of my banners and printing. This process and system allowed me to scale as many orders as needed without having to bear the burden of overhead myself.

Here are the benefits of brokering:

1. You can open multiple business channels in areas that you don't specialize in. You might not be good at doing web design, but you can find three web developers to represent. You can broker their services. You are a dealmaker, a sales person, and business developer.

2. You don't have to bear the monthly burden and expense of renting a brick-and-mortar building or pay for insurance, employees, and overhead. You can operate lean and provide the services with little effort. Force yourself to position life where you can work from a laptop anywhere in the world and have freedom.

3. Ego has a tendency to push you toward flash and prestige, like buildings with your name on them. Business trends go up and down and sales cycles do the same. You can insulate your lifestyle from these fluctuations by staying lean in your approach and systems.

Let's say your goal is to have a net income (the actual amount in your pocket at home) of $250,000. A great way to stretch yourself, and get into a position of living with options, is by leveraging the power of other's expertise. Hiring or brokering another who specializes in financial planning and strategy will often help you achieve your goals quicker and with less margin for error..

Your discipline (and challenge) is to keep your ego at bay from having to touch every aspect of the business. Let go to get more freedom, more money, and more growth.

Your role as an entrepreneur is to own businesses, not run them. Do you think that you're losing money if you hire a team or that you're making less because you broker a deal? Think again! Stop thinking in terms of what it will cost you and start thinking about how much more money you will make with all of the freedom you have.

If you were to restructure your approach in order to free yourself up to create more sales and grow the business, what changes would you make if you could broker, subcontract, or outsource? Would you sell your building? Partner with a competitor? Get radical in your thinking and rip the Band-Aid off? Better now than burning out or becoming overwhelmed.

Ask yourself this: If you were laid up in the hospital for three months, could your business continue without your presence?

Here's the reality: Get to a point where you make passive income on the efforts of someone else's expertise and efforts while you live in the sweet spot of making the deal and sale. Jeff Bezos of Amazon built an empire brokering other people's books and products. That is a perfect example of taking things you love to market without bearing the expense and overhead of each product's company. More importantly, if you're smart like Jeff, you'll do it virtually on the web, as there is no ceiling or capacity constraints online. The sky is the limit!

Have a great day.

29

Toys: Rent, Don't Buy

TOYS: RENT, DON'T BUY

In this world of consumerism, it often happens that all the stuff we own ends up owning us. Not only are we preoccupied with getting that cool new watch or car, but we end up spending more energy, time, and money maintaining, repairing, and keeping those things up to date. The items and products that we buy can steal our time. But it doesn't have to be this way.

I once talked with a millionaire about his choices when it came to his possessions. His answer was very interesting. He said that whenever he had the opportunity to purchase new experiences and large "toys" like motorcycles, jet skis, or motorhomes, he claimed that instead of buying them outright, he rents them. He went on to describe how this strategy has several surprising benefits. Here are a couple.

Get off the hook long-term: When it comes to boats, cars, houses, and recreational toys, it is easy to succumb to the lure of needing to just "have them." However, what most of us don't think about is the cost beyond the purchase—the major cost of maintenance.

I have seen people who make a good amount of money, yet they still live paycheck to paycheck because of their obsession with buying new stuff. Here's an example. I used to own a Harley. I loved riding it, but I had to store it, maintain it, and pay for the insurance, gas, and registration. I later sold it and put the money into our company. Now I rent one when I need it. The benefit is that I get to use a brand new model each time and then turn it in after I'm done without having to deal with it ever again.

Less to worry about: The more things we own, the more we have to manage. If you're a busy entrepreneur, having to manage ONE MORE THING might send you into a mild panic attack. I've learned that the best investments are in things that build value in relationships with loved ones and community. Everything else I rent. If you feel like all you're doing is managing a bunch of items that do nothing but cost you money and take up space, it might be a good idea to consider trimming the fat and freeing up bandwidth emotionally and financially.

Challenge: If you were to look at all of your possessions, is there anywhere you could trim the fat? What if you rented a vacation home instead of owning one? What if those saved dollars could be used to bless a family in need, start a new company or initiative, or help teach your kids through charity work?

The bottom line is this: Use it or lose it. Ask a couple of questions before making any kind of major purchase—what will it cost long-term and what fruit will ultimately come from it?

Have an amazing day!

———————————————

30

Make Customers the King

MAKE CUSTOMERS THE KING

I grew up in the music industry. One group of people that always fascinated me were the electronic composers—how they could "play" an entire room and pull at the emotions of their listeners. And perhaps one of the greatest places this is visible is at wedding receptions. Weddings are one of the most important days of our lives and everything hinges on the experience at the reception. The music can make or break the day. But have you ever been to a wedding that had a cheesy DJ or band at the reception?

During one particular wedding, I learned a big lesson by witnessing someone else's mistake. The wedding DJ was clearly only playing the songs that made him happy instead of giving the crowd what they wanted. The dance floor emptied, and what should have been a celebration quickly morphed into an uncomfortable environment.

As an entrepreneur and creative leader, it is paramount that you give your customers what they want. Whether you own a restaurant, a brick-and-mortar store, or an online ecommerce store, you're always playing with the art of selling to your customers. Let their needs and desires lead your choices. It takes a great deal of discipline to enforce this in your business, emails, campaigns, and marketing.

One of the surefire ways you can know you're hitting the target is when your customer says things like, "You're reading my mind," or "You're speaking my language." Our businesses are here to serve clients. However, there is one client who is the most important. In my thirty years of coaching entrepreneurs, the most costly blind spot is achieving your goals at the expense of your biggest customers: your spouse and your kids. As I have said in previous chapters, your spouse and family are your number one clients. Make sure they are served above everyone else.

We have no business going out to change the world if the world under our roof isn't transformed first.

Have an amazing day!

———————————————

31

Wisdom Is the Greatest Product You Will Ever Sell

WISDOM IS THE GREATEST
PRODUCT YOU WILL EVER SELL

One of the greatest crossroads an entrepreneur will encounter is what type of business to start or go into. But many neglect assessing their market, products, lifestyle, and preferences. Thus, the final discipline to adopt is the ability to hack your thinking and change your approach to determine the type of business you will invest in.

After thirty years of being an entrepreneur, I can tell you that I've experienced every kind of possible business. Whether it was custom painting clothes inside major department stores, selling my art on a Costco floor, hosting workshops, selling products online, or providing services, there is one product that trumps them all: wisdom. Or said another way: expertise.

My kids are both teenagers. As they grow into adulthood, I am doing everything possible to let them know the power of selling expertise—this should be on their radar as the greatest investment. I wish I would have known this thirty years ago. However, the Internet wasn't around. My life changed radically the moment I went into selling wisdom and expertise via online courses and modules. Here are a dozen of the many benefits:

1. No physical product.

2. No shelf life.

3. No inventory.

4. No physical building.

5. No staff; everything is automated.

6. No ceiling; you can take one order per day or thousands.

7. No limits; you can lead and operate your business on a laptop from anywhere in the world.

8. More quality time. You have the freedom to invest in your family.

9. More relationships. You can connect with a greater number of people on a deeper level.

10. More relevance. Your product is evergreen and never goes out of style.

11. More markets. You can provide as many products as you like and go into as many places as you like without overgrowing your building or platform.

12. More passion. You can nurture the many ideas you have in your heart to help people.

Often, the reply from many entrepreneurs is this, "I'm not an expert, and I don't have marketable wisdom." But the reality is you don't have to be an expert, and you will most certainly gain wisdom along the way if you are willing to be humble. Find the experts and present them to the world.

Wisdom is a product that gets better with time; the sooner you start selling and marketing wisdom, the sooner you can scale like you've never imagined. I'm not saying to stop everything you're doing and go into online business. What I am encouraging is for you to begin to supplement your current offering. You'll be glad you did. In the back of this book, I've provided ways we can connect if you'd like help on this journey.

Discipline yourself to invest in and create virtual businesses.

Have an amazing day.

NEXT STEPS

I hope that these last few weeks have allowed you to see life differently as it applies to your time, your talent, your craft, your career and relationships. My hope and prayer is that these disciplines will take root in your heart and soul to help you win.

Every day you have a choice to make. This choice is to determine if your time will be invested, wasted or spent. I want to help you make each day matter where you're not just adding scores to the scoreboard of life but also to your legacy both here and in eternity.

Moving forward, I would highly suggest that you form the habit of re-reading this book each morning before starting your day. You are what you eat. Downloading a dose of wisdom before heading into the challenges of the day will help equip your mind and soul. You'll be in the driver's seat. You might want more of what this book has to offer and desire to expand your leadership development. Would you like the opportunity to work personally with me? I have students worldwide whom I coach and mentor through my online platform.

Here are a couple of options and additional resources:

If you would like to discover, build and launch the brand of you, visit: www.noahuniversity.com

If you are looking to develop your influence and impact as a Christian leader in your business, family and relationships, visit: www.masters.life/start

---

No matter what, I would love to do life with you.

Take a moment to join my VIP email list by going to **www.noahelias.net**. You will receive my weekly videos, blogs and teachings to help you sharpen your creative edge.

If you want to go fast in life, go alone. If you want to go far, go together.
— ANCIENT PROVERB

I'm in your corner,

NOAH

"In the end, your life won't be measured or compared to others; you'll be measured based on the influence you had and the potential you possessed." - Bob Shank

_____